Help Me Be Good

Disobeying

Joy Berry
Illustrated by Bartholomew

Joy Berry Books
New York

This book is about Annie.

Reading about Annie can help you understand and deal with disobeying.

You are disobeying when you do not do what you have been told to do.

Your parents have good reasons for telling you what to do. This is why you should not disobey them.

Your parents tell you what to do because they do not want you to hurt yourself or others.

Your parents tell you what to do because
they do not want you to damage or destroy things.

Your parents tell you what to do because they want you to be liked by other people.

Your parents tell you what to do because they want you to be fair.

Sometimes you might wonder why parents get to tell their children what to do.

Parents tell their children what to do because they have lived longer and have learned more than children.

Thus, parents usually know what is best for their children.

Parents tell their children what to do because they are responsible for their children.

Parents have to take care of the damage when their children hurt themselves or others.

Sometimes parents need to punish their children for disobeying.

The purpose of a punishment is to make children feel bad about disobeying so they will not disobey again.

You can avoid being punished if you do these things:
- Talk to your parents.
- Find out what they want you to do. Then do it.

Sometimes you might not agree with your parents. Tell them how you feel.

They might change their minds. If they do not change their minds, drop the subject.

Nagging and throwing tantrums will only frustrate you and make your parents angry.

Tell the truth if you disobey.

Admit that you disobeyed.

Say that you are sorry and mean it.

Accept your punishment if you disobey.

Do not be angry at your parents when they punish you. Remember, it was you who disobeyed, not them.

Try not to disobey again.

When you obey, you please your parents, and you are doing what is best for you.

Joy Berry Enterprises
146 West 29th St., Suite 11RW
New York, NY 10001

Cover Design & Art Direction: John Bellaud
Cover Illustration & Art Production: Geoff Glisson

Publication Location: HX Printing, Guangzhou, China
Date of Production: February 2010
Cohort: Batch 1

Printed in China
ISBN 978-1-60577-137-3